# PRAYER

## worth
## repeating

Praying Together for
our Adult Children

Stonecroft

where she is ✛ as she is

STONECROFT
10561 Barkley, Suite 500
Overland Park, KS 66212
800.525.8627

ISBN: 978-0-9908500-1-4

Rev. 1014

# Contents

Friends,

Together we believe in the power of prayer because of the One we pray to—God Almighty. And while we won't know the entirety of the impact, our continual and repeated prayers make  a difference.

Prayer is, indeed, worth repeating.

We experience comfort, love, and the faithfulness of God as we submit our cares, our concerns, and yes, our children to the Lord.

This prayer devotional is designed for you—for you personally and for the time you spend praying together. As you pray for each other and for your children, look for God's hand at work and wait for His answers to your prayers. Be assured, He is at work in your life and in the lives of the ones you love.

> **"But blessed are those who trust in the LORD and have made the LORD their hope and confidence."**
>
> **—Jeremiah 17:7, NLT**

Together, we trust He hears us when we cry out to Him. May God bless you with hope and confidence as you faithfully and repeatedly lift your loved ones before His throne.

Stonecroft

# Why pray for your adult children?

A s the mother of adult children, you know that the "hands-on" stage of parenting is behind you. Yet your heart is just as connected to your children as when you had full oversight of their well-being. While you will always have a significant influence in their lives, your impact now takes a different shape. The purpose of this study is to connect mothers with God on behalf of their adult children who are not actively engaged with Him—moms who want to maximize their impact through the power of Scripture-focused prayer.

*Prayer Worth Repeating* provides women with a time and place for significant prayer. This resource offers inspiring devotionals and Scriptural prayer guidance, while you connect with women for powerful prayer. These women will encourage you to trust more deeply as God works in the lives of your adult children. This study provides space for you to journal your thoughts about the changes you see taking place within yourself, and your child, as you pray. Each mom will benefit having her own personal devotional guide to record and reveal how God answers her prayer.

*Prayer Worth Repeating* meets the needs of your group—whether you meet weekly, bi-weekly, or monthly. Just gather together a small group of women who share your desire to pray more effectively for their adult children. Meet where you'll be most comfortable and look forward to a time of focused praying and encouragement.

The personality of your group determines the format for your meetings. You may pray first or wait until after sharing the devotional together. You may use the Praying Scripture section at the end of each devotional to guide your group during prayer time, or as a personal resource between your group experiences—or both!

**PLACE A PHOTO OR PHOTOS OF YOUR CHILDREN HERE:**

# REALIGNING
## your mindset

## A Prayer Worth Repeating

The short, Old Testament book of Habakkuk creates the perfect place to pray for our adult children, though it's not very uplifting reading! The book begins with the nation of Judah in the midst of great turmoil. Habakkuk, one of God's faithful prophets, expresses great distress. In frustration he asks God, **"Where are you in all that's happening? Why aren't you paying attention to my prayers? How long before you do something about our circumstances?"** (see Habakkuk 1:1-4)

Sound familiar? How often have you been in Habakkuk's shoes—wondering if God will ever hear your cries, wondering why He seems to answer everyone else's prayers but not yours? This devastating place becomes especially frustrating when the prayers that seem to go unheard are those regarding your children.

➡ **What prayer for your child does God seem to be ignoring?**

Although we **know** God does not ignore us, it grows increasingly frustrating to watch the insidious passing of time with no sign of change in our child's life. That's when we need to remember and emulate Habakkuk's mindset! Although he begins the book in despair, and although God tells him things are going to get much worse before they get better, Habakkuk concludes with these powerful words of trust:

> **"Though the fig tree does not bud and there are no grapes on the vines, though the olive crop fails and the fields produce no food, though there are no sheep in the pen and no cattle in the stalls, yet I will rejoice in the LORD, I will be joyful in God my Savior. The Sovereign LORD is my strength; he makes my feet like the feet of a deer, he enables me to tread on the heights."**
>
> **—Habakkuk 3:17-19**

What an amazing, incredible, *empowering* mindset for us to embrace in the midst of our challenges! *Even though my world is crashing down around me, I am going to exalt in the Lord!*

In The Message, Habakkuk 3:19 is paraphrased: "I'm singing joyful praise to God. I'm turning cartwheels of joy to my Savior God. Counting on God's Rule to prevail, I take heart and gain strength. I run like a deer. I feel like I'm king of the mountain!"

Habakkuk understood *nothing* is gained from bemoaning the circumstances we find ourselves in. Not only is there nothing to be *gained*, but we risk a tremendous amount to be *lost*.

When our attention fixes on our circumstances—on everything going wrong—it distracts us from God. This creates for us a skewed sense of reality. It causes us to misinterpret the situation. We see the circumstances as large and insurmountable, producing in us a sense of hopelessness.

> **How do you alter your focus from your circumstances to God's perspective?**

Worship unlocks another perspective for us as mothers of adult children. When we choose to replace our concern and fear with a mindset of worship, we become more aware of God's heart—His fully devoted love for our children. When we align ourselves with God, who works from a higher plane than we can possibly imagine, we gain hope.

When our hearts despair that our prayers will never be answered, that is the very time to praise and worship God, who can do anything. The minute doubt-thoughts or fear-thoughts come to mind, determine to replace them with God-thoughts of worship, just as Habakkuk teaches us.

**Using Habakkuk's mindset of worship, write a personal prayer as it pertains to your child and then complete your prayer with the Scripture from Habakkuk:**

Though _____

And _____

Though _____

And _____

Though _____

And _____

**"Yet I will rejoice in the LORD, I will be joyful in God my Savior. The Sovereign LORD is my strength; he makes my feet like the feet of a deer, he enables me to tread on the heights."**

**—Habakkuk 3:18-19**

Repeat this personal prayer of worship throughout the week, trusting God every time your child comes to mind. Let it turn your focus toward God for whom nothing is impossible. Let it remind you that God's power and influence have no limits. There is no better thing you can do for your child than leave him in God's hands and worship God, despite your child's current circumstances.

Take time to list the names of the moms and their children, so you can faithfully pray for each other. (See the prayer list form on page 77.)

A PRAYER WORTH REPEATING          9

"I will pour out my Spirit on your offspring, and my blessing on your descendants. They will spring up like grass in a meadow, like poplar trees by flowing streams. Some will say, 'I belong to the Lᴏʀᴅ'; others will call themselves by the name of Jacob; still others will write on their hand, 'The Lᴏʀᴅ's,' and will take the name Israel."

## Praying Scripture - MYSELF

▶ Thank you, Father, that I don't have to be anxious for anything, but that in everything by prayer and petition, with thanksgiving, I can bring my requests to you; and that your peace, that transcends all understanding, will guard my heart and mind through Christ Jesus. (Philippians 4:6-7)

▶ Thank you, Lord, that when I pass through the waters, you will be with me; and through the rivers, they shall not sweep over me. When I walk through the fire, I will not be burned; the flames will not set me ablaze. (Isaiah 43:2)

▶ I do believe, Lord; help me overcome my unbelief. (Mark 9:24)

▶ Lord, you are my Rock and my Fortress and my Deliverer; my God, my Strength, in whom I will trust. (Psalm 18:2)

## Praying Scripture - MY CHILD

▶ Lord, I'm praying that my child will come to know you as Shepherd. (Psalm 23:1)

▶ Thank you, Father, that Jesus lives and always intercedes for my child. (Hebrews 7:25)

▶ Thank you, Lord, for the good work you have begun in my child and that you will carry on to completion. (Philippians 1:6)

# REFLECTIONS
REFLECTIONS

God has strengthened my confidence in Him by...

Today, I'm trusting these characteristics of God...

# REFLECTIONS

REFLECTIONS

# An Attitude Worth Developing

One mindset woven throughout the Bible that, when embraced, releases tremendous *power*. Intrinsic to this mindset is one word—*nevertheless*. Nevertheless shows up more than 90 times in the King James Version of the Bible, and 40 times in the New International Version. You might be surprised at the interesting things that accompany its use.

One of my favorite examples is in Luke 5:4-7 (KJV). Peter has been out fishing all night with a spectacular lack of success. He is exhausted and discouraged. Jesus comes along and tells him to let his net down one last time. It must have seemed like an exercise in futility to Peter, who replies, "Master, we have toiled all the night, and have taken nothing." Then, Peter seemingly adjusts his attitude. He sucks in a deep breath of determination and says, "Nevertheless at thy word I will let down the net."

He does, and his nets come up so bulging with fish they begin to break. In fact, Peter had to call another boat and its crew to come alongside to take some of the fish. There were so many fish, both boats began to sink!

There is such power hidden within a *nevertheless* attitude—one that trusts and obeys God, even against all reason; one that looks away from despair and discouragement and instead replies to God, *"Nevertheless, I will trust you!"*

➡️ **What circumstance surrounding your child is causing you the most anguish?**

Now read what you just wrote, and say to God, "Nevertheless, I will trust you!" In the days ahead, each time this circumstance comes to mind, address God again, "Nevertheless, I will trust you."

Psalm 77:7-14 is a wonderful example of the *nevertheless* attitude at work. The psalmist is filled with despair due to God's seeming abandonment of him:

➡ "Will the LORD reject forever? Will he never show his favor again? Has his unfailing love vanished forever? Has his promise failed for all time? Has God forgotten to be merciful? Has he in anger withheld his compassion?

"Then I thought, 'To this I will appeal: the years when the Most High stretched out his right hand. I will remember the deeds of the LORD; yes, I will remember your miracles of long ago. I will consider all your works and meditate on all your mighty deeds.

"Your ways, God, are holy. What god is as great as our God? You are the God who performs miracles; you display your power among the peoples.'"

As you read the verses following the psalmist's switch in focus, his lightened spirit is almost tangible. It builds with every verse. You can almost see the burden of his despair being lifted off his shoulders and transferred to the God who performs miracles.

➡ **Write about a time when you experienced God at work in your life.**

Become like the psalmist. Create a habit of reflecting on the goodness God creates in your life and the life of your child and rely upon those times as you continue to pray for your child. Practice shifting your focus from an apparent lack of activity of God, to all He has done. Your faith will be strengthened.

➡ **List a handful of times you've seen God undertake for your child: answers to prayer, interventions, safety. Share with the group and take time to praise God for His activity in your child's life.**

When you explore your current situation, especially when the very life of your child is at stake, it sometimes takes tremendous faith to believe God overrides the stark reality of the facts. It is difficult to look at your child, who is not engaged with God, and believe *this situation is nothing compared to God*. Nevertheless, whatever circumstance your child is in, God is greater!

Set your mind to develop a *nevertheless* attitude in regard to your child.

When you get discouraging news, *nevertheless* trust God.

When you despair of ever again seeing a sign of progress, *nevertheless* trust God.

When you want to give up in impatience, *nevertheless* trust God.

He is trustworthy. He is greater.

## Scripture Focus: Psalms 77:14

**"You are the God who performs miracles; you display your power among the peoples."**

## Praying Scripture – MYSELF

▶ Father, help me to be strong in you and in your mighty power. Let me put on the full armor of God, so that I can stand strong against all of Satan's schemes. (Ephesians 6:10-11)

▶ Father, thank you that you go before me and my family, and that you fight for us. (Deuteronomy 1:30)

## Praying Scripture – MY CHILD

▶ I ask that you will seek my child who has gone astray like a lost sheep, and that you will not let him forget your commandments. (Psalm 119:176)

▶ Father, cause my child to turn back to you and let her experience your mercy and wonderful forgiveness. (Isaiah 55:7)

▶ Thank you that when my child calls on you, you will be faithful and just and will forgive him and purify him from all unrighteousness. (1 John 1:9)

▶ I ask that you will open my children's eyes and turn them from darkness to light, and from the power of Satan to you, God. (Acts 26:18a)

# REFLECTIONS
REFLECTIONS

God has strengthened my confidence in Him by...

Today, I'm trusting these characteristics of God...

# A Perspective Worth Maintaining

In 2 Kings 6, a story appears of a sure disaster in the making. The king of Syria, in his anger against Elisha, sets up an ambush against the city where Elisha is staying. During the night he sends horses, chariots, and an army of men to surround the city.

When Elisha's servant gets up early the next morning and sees that they are surrounded, he cries out in fear, "Oh no, my lord, what shall we do?"

Has such a panic-stricken thought ever crossed your mind regarding your child? *Lord, what am I going to do?* It certainly has mine.

I love Elisha's calm answer: "'Don't be afraid,' the prophet answered. 'Those who are with us are more than those who are with them!'" (2 Kings 6:16).

Elisha then asked God to open his servant's eyes to see the truth of the situation. Suddenly the servant got a glimpse of the spiritual realm surrounding them. It's the same spiritual realm that surrounds us. The servant saw the hills were full of horses and chariots of fire (see 2 Kings 6:14-17).

Now, nothing about the situation changed. Elisha and his servant were still surrounded by a fierce and terrifying enemy army. The servant's understanding of the facts changed. Once his spiritual eyes were opened, he was able to see more about what had always been true:

God is bigger.

God is mightier.

God is far stronger than any army that would ever come against them.

*Nothing and no one outnumbers God!*

Oh, the wonder of those words that Elisha spoke to his servant: "Those who are with us are more than those who are with them!"

And still true today.

There is no force in this world greater than God. Whatever surrounds your child today cannot compare to the power of God! God pursues your child with power and love. Meditate on God's magnificent and unmatchable power.

➡ **What do you picture when you think about God pursing your child?**

Elisha chose to believe in the power he saw at work in the spiritual realm. The Israelites, however, chose to believe in the power they saw at work in the physical realm.

God had promised them a land of their own. He told them they had nothing to fear, that He would see to it they had victory every step of the way. But when they heard reports of giants living in the land, their faith transferred from the power of God to the power of the giants. (see Numbers 13:25 – 14:4)

➡ **What about you? How will you exhibit more faith in the power of God in your child's life?**

It can be very difficult to keep believing God's overriding power rather than the world's influence, when it seems He has no part in your child's life. The truth is that God has a terrific influence in your child's life even though your child may ignore Him. God is active even when your child does not respond. Nevertheless, it is crucial that you keep your mind set on God's unmatchable, active power. Refuse to slide into the position the Israelites did when God asked Moses, "How long will these people treat me with contempt? How long will they refuse to believe in me, in spite of all the signs I have performed among them?" (see Numbers 14:11)

**Regardless of the facts surrounding your child, the truth is God is not limited by those facts. List some facts about your child and beside each fact write a truth about God. For example:**

| Fact: | Scripture-Based Truth: |
|---|---|
| My child does not have a relationship with God. | God is not willing that any should perish. |

**Scripture Focus: Hebrews 11:6**

**"And without faith it is impossible to please God, because anyone who comes to him must believe that he exists and that he rewards those who earnestly seek him."**

## Praying Scripture – MYSELF

▶ Father, I know that you are not slow in keeping your promise, as some understand slowness. You are patient, not wanting anyone to perish, but everyone to come to repentance. (2 Peter 3:9)

▶ Thank you Lord, that your love reaches to the heavens, your faithfulness to the skies. (Psalms 36:5)

## Praying Scripture – MY CHILD

▶ Father, open my child's eyes and turn her from darkness to light, and from the power of Satan to God, so that she may receive forgiveness of sins and a place among those who are sanctified by faith in Jesus Christ. (Acts 26:18)

▶ Lord, I pray that my child will put off his former way of life, to be made new in the attitude of his mind; and to put on the new self, created to be like God in true righteousness and holiness. (Ephesians 4:22-24)

▶ Father, thank you for not letting my foot slip—and that you, who watch over my child, will not slumber. (Psalms 121:3)

# REFLECTIONS
REFLECTIONS

God has strengthened my confidence in Him by...

Today, I'm trusting these characteristics of God...

# FIXING YOUR FOCUS
## on the end result

## Against All Odds

**N**e of the Bible's most amazing stories of victory in spite of tremendous odds surrounds a young man named Gideon (Judges 6 and 7). When Gideon first appears in the book of Judges, he and all the Israelites are hiding from the Midianites, who have been terrorizing them for years. When God calls Gideon to lead his people to freedom, Gideon's first response is disbelief—the circumstances appear impossible. God remains steadfast, however, and Gideon finally gathers together a band of men willing to go up against their fearsome foe.

Incredibly, God tells Gideon his army is too big.

God whittles their numbers until just 300 of them are left to go up against the mighty Midianite army of 120,000 soldiers. Gideon's story begins on a hopeless note, and God *appears* to make it even more hopeless. Pure craziness! Do you ever feel, in spite of your many prayers for your child, things seem to go from bad to worse?

➡ **What circumstances in your child's life do you see as being the biggest barrier to her engaging fully with Christ?**

➡ **What part of your child's life choices and/or attitude do you find most threatening to your ability to trust God to bring him into active faith in Jesus Christ?**

God shows incredible patience with Gideon's lack of confidence and faith that his people would ever again be free. God is also patient with you when your confidence wavers regarding your child. He continually reassured Gideon.

To bolster his confidence, God tells Gideon to sneak down to the Midianite encampment the night before the battle and eavesdrop on a conversation between two soldiers. Read what happened in Judges 7:13-15:

> **"Gideon arrived just as a man was telling a friend his dream. 'I had a dream,' he was saying. 'A round loaf of barley bread came tumbling into the Midianite camp. It struck the tent with such force that the tent overturned and collapsed.'**

> **"His friend responded, 'This can be nothing other than the sword of Gideon son of Joash, the Israelite. God has given the Midianites and the whole camp into his hands.'**

> **"When Gideon heard the dream and its interpretation, he bowed down and worshipped. He returned to the camp of Israel and called out, 'Get up! The LORD has given the Midianite camp into your hands.'"**

Look at this passage again. Gideon did two things after hearing the conversation.

> **What is the first thing Gideon did after hearing the conversation between the two Midianite soldiers?**

To understand the significance of this, you need to get a picture of where Gideon was when he suddenly dropped to his knees to worship God. Read Judges 7:12:

> **"The Midianites, the Amalekites and all the other eastern peoples had settled in the valley, thick as locusts. Their camels could no more be counted than the sand on the seashore."**

The enemy's numbers are innumerable—too many to count. Yet, right there outside one of the soldier's tents, Gideon decided to have a prayer meeting! Smack in the middle of enemy territory, he took time to acknowledge the One who was directing the miraculous circumstances of his life.

When we decide to position ourselves to worship Almighty God, even in enemy territory, we step into the realm of the miraculous.

We place ourselves in the presence of the Creator of the universe! We stand in the shadow of Perfection and Wisdom and Mercy and Compassion and Love.

As we give God our full attention, we experience His full attention. Begin to comprehend the wonder of this.

➡️ **Take a moment to write down your thoughts and responses to God giving you His full attention.**

➡️ **What is the second thing Gideon did?**

Gideon proclaims victory—*even before they set out for the battlefield!* "Get up!" he tells his men. "The LORD has given the Midianite camp into your hands." When he proclaimed victory in advance, Gideon believed that what God said was true—he was proclaiming his faith and confidence in God. He sets his mind not on *his* ability, but on God's faithfulness to do what He said. Our faith is important in seeing God at work.

Picture what you are longing to see happen with your child. If your child ever walked in close relationship with God, remember those times as you pray. Thank God that He longs to see your child worship Him again.

**Scripture Focus: Jeremiah 32:38-41**

**"They will be my people, and I will be their God. I will give them singleness of heart and action, so that they will always fear me and that all will then go well for them and for their children after them. I will make an everlasting covenant with them: I will never stop doing good to them, and I will inspire them to fear me, so that they will never turn away from me. I will rejoice in doing them good and will assuredly plant them in this land with all my heart and soul."**

---

### Praying Scripture – MYSELF

▶ Thank you Father, that you will do immeasurably more than all that I ask or imagine according to your power that is at work in me. (Ephesians 3:20)

▶ Oh Father, your righteousness reaches to the skies, and you have done great things. (Psalm 71:19)

▶ How wonderful Father, that I don't have to fight this battle. All I have to do is stand firm and see the deliverance you are going to bring. Thank you for telling me not to be afraid or discouraged, because you are with me. (2 Chronicles 20:17)

### Praying Scripture – MY CHILD

▶ Thank you that in all things my child may be more than a conqueror through you who love him. (Romans 8:37)

▶ Thank you that my child, when she believes, will see the exceeding greatness of your power toward her, according to the working of your mighty power. (Ephesians 1:19)

▶ Father, become a strong refuge for my child and a strong Tower from the enemy. (Psalm 61:3)

# REFLECTIONS
REFLECTIONS

God has strengthened my confidence in Him by...

Today, I'm trusting these characteristics of God...

# REFLECTIONS

REFLECTIONS

_____
_____
_____
_____
_____
_____
_____
_____
_____
_____
_____
_____
_____
_____
_____
_____
_____
_____
_____
_____
_____
_____
_____
_____
_____
_____
_____
_____

# An Image More Like Christ

Joseph was a kid with issues. He held an inflated image of himself. His father made it obvious that Joseph was the favored child. To exacerbate matters, God's gift to Joseph to interpret dreams set him apart even more. In his youthful arrogance, Joseph mishandled the gift. He told his brothers that according to his dreams, they were one day going to bow down to him. This wasn't a wise thing to say to siblings!

Joseph's arrogance, combined with the jealousy and hatred of his brothers, produced disastrous consequences. The dysfunction in this family became so out-of-control that Joseph's brothers plotted his murder. However, they settled for something less drastic and sold him off to a band of slave traders on their way to Egypt.

Don't you wonder what Joseph's thoughts were as he watched his brothers take money in exchange for him and his freedom?

What do you think his thoughts were later in Egypt when, after being such a trustworthy slave to Potiphar, he landed in prison because of Potiphar's lying wife?

What about later when his fellow prisoner, whom he had helped, forgot his promise to remember Joseph?

For more than a dozen years, Joseph's life was a seesaw of wild highs and devastating lows. Joseph never could have grasped how God would use those years of preparation. (Read about Joseph in Genesis chapters 37 and 39-47.)

➡️ **What are some of the significant highs and lows of your child's life?**

What does this have to do with your child? Simply this: God used every single twist and turn in Joseph's life for His purpose. Not for a minute was Joseph ever out of God's reach. And your child isn't out of God's reach either.

In every circumstance Joseph found himself in, his gift for leadership emerged. Just as God equipped Joseph with gifts and abilities, He has equipped your child.

In the beginning, Joseph misused his gift and it cost him dearly. It took a long season of both slavery and imprisonment to refine and prepare Joseph for the specific assignment God had for him. The result, however, was a man so yielded to God that Pharaoh entrusted everything to him—his personal household, the workings of the country—everything. Joseph's power and influence were remarkable for a foreigner who arrived in the country as a slave. God used prison in Joseph's life.

Like Joseph's situation, God can use every person's circumstance to bring Him glory.

Like Joseph, God equips each of us with the abilities and gifting we need to fulfill His plan.

➡️ **Take a moment and contemplate your child's gifting and God's plan for him. Think big!**

Thank God for ways He has gifted your child and for the work He is doing in your child's life, even if it is not visible to you. Trust God with the end result He wants for your child—an image more like Jesus.

God knows how to draw your child to Himself. Trust God with the current details of your child's life. Expect Him to work good out of it. The many twists in Joseph's life eventually led to him being in a position to save his brothers' lives. By the time that remarkable opportunity presented itself, Joseph was a changed man. There was no hint of bitterness or desire for vengeance—nothing that stemmed from the evil his brothers intended for him. Instead there was a man transformed into the image of Christ, a man filled with gratitude for being reunited with his family. God works in your child's life, too. We can thank God and ask Him to complete the good work He has begun.

"And we know that in all things God works for the good of those who love him, who have been called according to his purpose. For those God foreknew he also predestined to be conformed to the image of his Son, that he might be the firstborn among many brothers and sisters."

## Praying Scripture – MYSELF

▶ Father, help me to walk by faith and not by sight. (2 Corinthians 5:7)

▶ Thank you, Lord, that I am strengthened in my faith. I praise you, because I am fully persuaded that you have the power to do what you have promised. (Romans 4:20-21)

## Praying Scripture – MY CHILD

▶ Father, thank you for the plans you have for my child's life, plans to prosper her and not to harm her, plans to give my child a hope and a future. (Jeremiah 29:11)

▶ Father, I pray that you will be manifested in my child's life, so that you will destroy the works of Satan. (1 John 3:8)

▶ Father, I pray that my child will cease giving a foothold to Satan. (Ephesians 4:27)

▶ Father, cause my child to hate evil, guard his life and deliver him from the hand of the wicked. (Psalm 97:10)

# REFLECTIONS
REFLECTIONS

_____

_____

_____

_____

_____

_____

_____

_____

God has strengthened my confidence in Him by...

_____

_____

_____

_____

_____

_____

_____

Today, I'm trusting these characteristics of God...

_____

_____

_____

_____

_____

_____

_____

_____

_____

_____

# Your Heart's Desire

ne of my favorite of the many notable Sir Winston Churchill quotes is, "You cannot tell from appearances how things will go. Sometimes imagination makes things out far worse than they are."

Although he was not speaking to the art of parenting, his words here are applicable to mothers. Oh, how easily our imaginations can get the best of us! How effortlessly we can look at a situation and see the worst. The Israelites had the same tendency. Read Numbers 13:26-33:

> **"They came back to Moses and Aaron and the whole Israelite community at Kadesh in the Desert of Paran. There they reported to them and to the whole assembly and showed them the fruit of the land. They gave Moses this account: 'We went into the land to which you sent us, and it does flow with milk and honey! Here is its fruit. But the people who live there are powerful, and the cities are fortified and very large. We even saw descendants of Anak there. The Amalekites live in the Negev; the Hittites, Jebusites and Amorites live in the hill country; and the Canaanites live near the sea and along the Jordan.'**

> **"Then Caleb silenced the people before Moses and said, 'We should go up and take possession of the land, for we can certainly do it.'**

> **"But the men who had gone up with him said, 'We can't attack those people; they are stronger than we are.' And they spread among the Israelites a bad report about the land they had explored. They said, 'The land we explored devours those living in it. All the people we saw there are of great size. We saw the Nephilim there (the descendants of Anak come from the Nephilim). We seemed like grasshoppers in our own eyes, and we looked the same to them.'"**

Do you remember what Churchill said? Something about not being able to predict the future accurately from the present appearances; how our imagination can make things out far worse than they really are? The Israelites were masters of "expecting the worst," but nothing good comes from such an outlook. Read what God had to say about their attitude in Numbers 14:21-23:

➡️ **"Nevertheless, as surely as I live and as surely as the glory of the Lord fills the whole earth, not one of those who saw my glory and the signs I performed in Egypt and in the wilderness but who disobeyed me and tested me ten times—not one of them will ever see the land I promised on oath to their ancestors. No one who has treated me with contempt will ever see it."**

Those are heartbreaking words spoken by God. His desire was to shower His children with magnificent blessings.

➡️ **When do you struggle with the same inability to trust God?**

➡️ **Have you ever stopped to consider how your lack of trust might be preventing you from living a more faithful life? Write out your thoughts.**

God wants to help you increase your trust in Him. He knows that trust takes practice. Your child's current lack of engagement with God offers the perfect opportunity for you to practice trusting Him.

Think about this: Joshua and Caleb saw the very same things the other spies saw. They saw all the same giants and the same massive, fortified cities. But they viewed what they saw through the eyes of faith—that God had given them *ownership*. There might be giants living there, but that land belonged to them! After their long, treacherous journey out of slavery, they at last looked upon the magnificent land God promised them. God was not surprised or concerned that giants lived there. He knew that fact from even before He promised that same land to His children. He was not surprised at the large, fortified cities, either.

Similarly, your child's spiritual state does not surprise God. You have no power over your child's choices, or the philosophies he embraces, or the lifestyles he adopts. So, stop worrying about him. Instead, view your child through God's eyes. Meditate on the plans God has for your child, the very plans He laid out even before He laid the foundations of the world. Thank God for how He knit your child together in the womb and numbered his days before his first breath of earthly air.

 **Write out a prayer for your child's future:**

Another of Churchill's quotes is, "Never give in. Never give in. Never, never, never, never. Never yield to the apparently overwhelming might of the enemy."

Take those words to heart concerning your child. Don't give any consideration to the *apparently* overwhelming might of the enemy. Give all consideration to the *assured*, overwhelming might of God!

"Whoever dwells in the shelter of the Most High will rest in the shadow of the Almighty. I will say of the Lord, "He is my refuge and my fortress, my God, in whom I trust.""

## Praying Scripture – MYSELF

▶ Father, help my light to shine before my child, that he will see my good deeds and praise you in heaven. (Matthew 5:16)

▶ Thank you for the confidence I can have in approaching you: that if I ask anything according to your will, you will hear me. (1 John 5:14-15)

▶ Thank you for being my confidence and for keeping my feet from slipping. (Proverbs 3:26)

## Praying Scripture – MY CHILD

▶ Lord, let my child humble himself under your mighty hand, and I trust you to lift him up in due time. (1 Peter 5:6)

▶ Lord, let my child hear and listen to your voice; let my child follow you. Give her eternal life so she shall never perish, and no one can snatch her out of your hand. (John 10:27-28)

▶ Father, I know you are able to keep my child from falling and that you are able to present him before your glorious presence without fault and with great joy. (Jude 1:24)

# REFLECTIONS
REFLECTIONS

God has strengthened my confidence in Him by...

Today, I'm trusting these characteristics of God...

# REFLECTIONS

# TRUSTING GOD
## with the shape of His answer

## Where is Your Focus?

The way we pray may set us up for disappointment with God. Disappointment is the last emotion we should experience when we pray, and yet we encounter it. When we become so focused on our desired outcome of our prayer that God becomes secondary, when He becomes the means to our desired end, disappointment follows.

This subtle shift in focus can cause us to fail to recognize God's hand at work in our child's life when the evidence does not line up with our desired answer. Sadly, this sometimes can cause distance in our relationship with God.

God works from an unlimited perspective in time. We cannot see beyond the precise moment we exist in right now, today, at this hour, during this minute. But God's perspective covers all of eternity! He sees this moment, but He also sees tomorrow, next week, seven months from now, two years from now, three decades from now. When we remember this, our focus on God, rather than on the desired outcome of our prayers, is the only course to take.

When viewed from your limited perspective, your child's life might appear to be completely in the grips of the world. When viewed circumstance by circumstance, choice by choice, it might seem as if God is completely shut out. Nevertheless, the Bible tells us in Proverbs 16:4 that, "The LORD works out everything for his own ends" (NIV 1984). Think about that for a minute.

➡ **What does this verse say to you regarding your child's current situation?**

Immense gratitude and relief overwhelm me as I contemplate this verse. *Think of it!* Almighty God, with no limitations whatsoever, who loves your child far more than you do, is working everything out for His own ends. Does it not make sense then, to release your desires for your child and simply embrace God?

God's will flows through *all* circumstances. His work in one circumstance sets the stage for the next. Throughout your life some circumstances will always seem completely contrary to what you pray for. But the longer you walk with God, the more evidence you will gather that demonstrates again and again how that one circumstance that brought such disappointment or heartbreak actually serves as the catalyst for the next circumstance that signifies victory.

Here is the truth: Your child's current spiritual apathy is not the end of the story! God actively works in her life today. Read Psalm 73:21-26 with yourself in mind:

> **"When my heart was grieved and my spirit embittered, I was senseless and ignorant; I was a brute beast before you. Yet I am always with you; you hold me by my right hand. You guide me with your counsel, and afterward you will take me into glory. Who have I in heaven but you? And earth has nothing I desire besides you. My flesh and my heart may fail, but God is the strength of my heart and my portion forever."**

> **Underline the most important phrase in this passage to you today. Share it with the group.**

Even in your grief over your child's current situation, even though you may experience bitterness as a result of God's perceived lack of attention to your prayers, still He is always with you. He holds your hand and gives you counsel. He is all you'll ever need.

Determine right now to let go of your desired answer for your child and focus on God, your portion forever.

> **Write out your statement of determination.**

Read Psalm 73:21-26 again. This time, consider your child as you read.

Even though, right this moment, your child may be spiritually "senseless and ignorant," God is always with her. God is all your child will ever need and He will be her portion forever. Pray these verses over your child. Give her to God again, and trust Him with the shape of His answer.

**Scripture Focus: Psalms 73:25-26**

**"Whom have I in heaven but you? And earth has nothing I desire besides you. My flesh and my heart may fail, but God is the strength of my heart and my portion forever."**

## Praying Scripture – MYSELF

▶ Lord, keep me in perfect peace by keeping my mind focused on you, because I trust in you. (Isaiah 26:3)

▶ Father, fill me with all joy and peace as I trust in you, so that I may overflow with hope by the power of your Holy Spirit. (Romans 15:13)

▶ Thank you that in all things we are more than conquerors through you who love us. (Romans 8:37)

## Praying Scripture – MY CHILD

▶ Father, let my child kneel before you, from whom the whole family in heaven and on Earth derives its name. Strengthen my child with power through your Spirit, so that Christ may dwell in her heart through faith. Let my child be rooted and established in love, give her power, together with all the saints, so that she can grasp how wide and long and high and deep is Christ's love, and will know this love that surpasses knowledge—that she may be filled to the measure of all the fullness of God. (Ephesians 3:14-19)

▶ Father, bring the great peace to my child that comes from loving your law, so that nothing can make him stumble. (Psalm 119:165)

# REFLECTIONS
REFLECTIONS

_____
_____
_____
_____
_____
_____
_____
_____

God has strengthened my confidence in Him by...
_____
_____
_____
_____
_____
_____
_____

Today, I'm trusting these characteristics of God...
_____
_____
_____
_____
_____
_____
_____
_____
_____

# Releasing Your Desired Outcome to God

Have you ever questioned the way God answered your prayers? Have you ever felt completely ignored by God? Though the Bible assures us of God's omnipresence, have you sometimes felt He has taken a break from where you are? That He was far? I think we all have. And I think we all have, at one time or another, been devastated by the question, "Why?"

"Why did you allow this to happen, God?"

"Why didn't you protect my family?"

"Why didn't you heal my child?"

"Why didn't you solve my problem?"

The more desperate our prayers, the stronger our guard should be against the potential for disappointment or disillusionment. Even as we pray, we expect a certain outcome. We have the shape of God's answer already formed in our mind. Thus our prayers become not so much a "releasing to God," but rather a telling God what He should do on our behalf, or even on behalf of our child. In truth, it is our not-so-subtle way of retaining control.

➡️ **What are some of the "suggestions" you've given God as to how your prayers for your child should be answered?**

Read Philippians 4:6-9:

▶ **"Do not be anxious about anything, but in every situation, by prayer and petition, with thanksgiving, present your requests to God. And the peace of God, which transcends all understanding, will guard your hearts and your minds in Christ Jesus.**

**"Finally, brothers and sisters, whatever is true, whatever is noble, whatever is right, whatever is pure, whatever is lovely, whatever is admirable—if anything is excellent or praiseworthy—think about such things. Whatever you have learned or received or heard from me, or seen in me—put it into practice. And the God of peace will be with you."**

▶ **What is the very first thing this passage tells you to do?**

▶ **How should you present your requests to God?**

Thanksgiving is essential in our prayer life. An attitude of thanksgiving to God, regardless of what we face, keeps everything in right balance. Thanksgiving protects us from disappointment and disillusionment as it locks our focus on God instead of our problem. Thanksgiving enables us to trust Him with the details. Praise is a vital part of praying for our children. It reminds us that God is in charge and that He is capable.

Read Philippians 4:6-9 in Eugene Peterson's paraphrase of the Bible, *The Message*:

▶ **"Don't fret or worry. Instead of worrying, pray. Let petitions and praises shape your worries into prayers, letting God know your concerns. Before you know it, a sense of God's wholeness, everything coming together for good, will come and settle you down. It's wonderful what happens when Christ displaces worry at the center of your life.**

**"Summing it all up, friends, I'd say you'll do best by filling your minds and meditating on things true, noble, reputable, authentic, compelling, gracious—the best, not the worst; the beautiful, not the ugly; things to praise, not things to curse. Put into practice what you learned from me, what you heard and saw and realized. Do that, and God, who makes everything work together, will work you into his most excellent harmonies."**

Let your praises shape your worries into prayers. The more we worship God, the more we praise Him, the better shape our prayers take.

➡ **What does this passage say the result of our praise will be?**

Don't you love the thought of God putting a guard around your mind, blocking relentless worry from entering your life and setting up camp? How wonderful to know He wants to displace your worries and fears with His peace!

Again, before you know it, a sense of God's wholeness comes and settles you down. Take a moment and let God settle you down in regard to your child. Lean against Him and take a deep breath. Listen to Him whisper to you.

➡ **Reflect on this and write your thoughts.**

Worry seems to be a natural state for moms, doesn't it? It's very difficult to maintain a constant mindset of peace when your child is not where you want him to be.

➡ **What is Paul's God-inspired recommendation in this passage for keeping our negative thoughts at bay?**

To meditate on something means to give it your full attention, to examine it from every angle, and to block out all distractions. In order to truly fill up your mind with good things when you're in the midst of distress, you need to prepare in advance. The Apostle Paul tells us exactly how to do this.

➡️ **Write out the list of things we are told to fill our mind with. Then, consider and write what you are going to turn your thoughts to in regard to your child. For example:**

Things that are true about my child:     God is watching over her every step.

Things that are noble about my child:     He is honest.

_____     _____

_____     _____

_____     _____

_____     _____

_____     _____

When you return home, copy this list down on a separate piece of paper or card, so you have it handy. Then, when you start to worry or allow a negative thought to enter your mind, look at the list and fill your mind with the thoughts you've written down. Praise God for what you've written. If you do this consistently, you will begin to discover something truly amazing.

➡️ **According to the last verse in the passage, what is it?**

The God of peace will be with you! Faith will displace your worry! God will indulge your insecurities. He understands how hard it is to give Him full control, and He will reward even your smallest effort to think on the good things.

Thank Him right now for putting a guard around your mind. Let Him again settle you down and fill you with His peace.

**"What, then, shall we say in response to these things? If God is for us, who can be against us? He who did not spare his own Son, but gave him up for us all—how will he not also, along with him, graciously give us all things?"**

---

## Praying Scripture – MYSELF

▶ Father, let your peace rule my heart in all things. (Colossians 3:15)

▶ Father, I cast all my cares on you for I know you care for me. (1 Peter 5:7)

▶ Father, when I lie down I know I do not have to be afraid and my sleep will be sweet. (Proverbs 3:24)

▶ Father, I will not fear, for you are with me. I will not be dismayed, for you are my God. you strengthen me and help me and uphold me with your righteous right hand. (Isaiah 41:10)

## Praying Scripture – MY CHILD

▶ Father, let my child know that every word of yours is flawless and that you are a shield to those who put their trust in you. (Proverbs 30:5)

▶ Father, let my child become your servant; give him discernment, so that he will understand your statutes. (Psalm 119:125)

# REFLECTIONS

God has strengthened my confidence in Him by...

Today, I'm trusting these characteristics of God...

# Why vs. Who

**J**ob was a man fully committed to God. Nothing distracted him from that commitment—not the destruction of his livelihood and wealth, not the death of his family, not the loss of his health. However, as his distress reached unbearable proportions, he did question God. Questioning God is a natural response when adversity piles up.

**What questions have you asked, or are asking, God regarding your child?**

God has compassion on our questions that arise from the depth of our sorrow and pain. We see God's compassion in the way He responded to Job's questions. When that devastated, wounded, utterly broken man looked up at God and asked "Why?" God did not give Job a direct answer. He did not say, "Well, Job, Satan wanted to put your love for me to the test, and since you are such an honorable man, I agreed to let him do whatever he wanted to you, except take your life."

Our all-wise God knew such a response, even though technically the correct answer to Job's question, would not have comforted or soothed him. Instead of answering Job directly, God responded with a series of His own questions, something like this:

*"Job," He asked, "where were you when I was laying the earth's foundations? Have you ever commanded the morning to appear or robed the dawn in red? Can you ensure the proper sequence of the seasons? Can you make lightning to appear and cause it to strike as you direct it?"*

On and on and on, through two entire chapters of the Bible (Job 38-39) God continues to ask such questions, all designed to show His sovereignty compared to Job's frailty. At first glance, God's response doesn't appear to be compassionate. It sounds like He's saying, *"Job, who do you think you are to question me? I'm God. I can do whatever I want."*

However, as we read these chapters carefully and repeatedly, and as we let the utter majesty and ability of God wash over us, then we will begin to see that God's questions to Job actually formed the most compassionate response He could have offered him. In essence He seems to say, *"Job, look at me, look at my power, my ability, my wisdom. Look at all that I have done, and have the power to do. If I can do all this—create the whole world and keep it running every second of the day—then don't you see you can trust me to take care of you! There is nothing I can't do, no problem I can't solve, no pain I can't ease."*

God reminds Job that He operates from a position of omniscience—past, present, future. Job was locked in his moment of excruciating pain. He could not see the future awaiting him, arranged by God, whose love cannot be measured or altered. *What an incredibly loving answer to give a man in such severe physical and psychological pain*—to prove to him beyond a shadow of a doubt that God holds all things in His hand, including Job and the devastation he was experiencing.

God's answer to Job thousands of years ago remains valid today. When questions rise within you, when thoughts of "why?" crash down on you, fix your focus on the "who" of your circumstances. There's only the difference of one letter between the question "why?" and "who?" but there's a vast difference in the answer. "Why?" creates doubts; "who?" creates confidence.

**➡ Jot down several truths about God that strengthen your confidence in Him.**

Whatever questions you're asking God, don't lose sight of the fact that the God who causes the sun to rise every single morning, who keeps the Earth spinning on its axis, is the very same God who watches over your child. Let go of your *why* and embrace the *who*. Worship Almighty God.

**"Because I know whom I have believed, and am convinced that he is able to guard what I have entrusted to him until that day."**

## Praying Scripture – MYSELF

▶ Father, I know that you are the Lord my God and there is no other. (Joel 2:27)

▶ I know that you are the First and the Last; apart from you there is no God. (Isaiah 44:6)

## Praying Scripture – MY CHILD

▶ Thank you for loving my child with an everlasting love and drawing her to you with loving-kindness. (Jeremiah 31:3)

▶ Lord, I know that you are faithful, and I ask that you will strengthen my child and protect him from the evil one. (2 Thessalonians 3:3)

▶ Thank you, Father, that neither death nor life, neither angels nor demons, neither the present nor the future, nor any powers, neither height nor depth, nor anything else in all creation, will be able to separate my child from your love. (Romans 8:38-39)

# REFLECTIONS
REFLECTIONS

_____
_____
_____
_____
_____
_____
_____
_____
_____
_____

God has strengthened my confidence in Him by...
_____
_____
_____
_____
_____
_____
_____
_____

Today, I'm trusting these characteristics of God...
_____
_____
_____
_____
_____
_____
_____
_____
_____
_____
_____

# GOD'S TIMING
## is perfect

## Waiting: A Different Perspective

s there anything more discouraging than waiting—especially with no end in sight? When the time of waiting surrounds a child for whom you are praying, the waiting seems especially discouraging. But have you ever wondered how God views this time of waiting? Read Romans 8:22-28:

**"We know that the whole creation has been groaning as in the pains of childbirth right up to the present time. Not only so, but we ourselves, who have the firstfruits of the Spirit, groan inwardly as we wait eagerly for our adoption to sonship, the redemption of our bodies. For in this hope we were saved. But hope that is seen is no hope at all. Who hopes for what they already have? But if we hope for what we do not yet have, we wait for it patiently.**

**"In the same way, the Spirit helps us in our weakness. We do not know what we ought to pray for, but the Spirit himself intercedes for us through wordless groans. And he who searches our hearts knows the mind of the Spirit, because the Spirit intercedes for God's people in accordance with the will of God.**

**"And we know that in all things God works for the good of those who love him, who have been called according to his purpose."**

What an incredible picture—comparing waiting to pregnancy! Pregnancy brings new life, new beginnings. During those nine months of waiting, tremendous growth takes place, internally and externally. And the process leaves you forever changed. Your body is never the same again, your mind is never the same again, your heart is never the same again. The waiting enlarged you physically and emotionally in ways you never imagined.

How do the effects of waiting change your attitude in regard to your prayers for your child? Does it temper your impatience with expectancy and anticipation? Does it fill you with a sense of wonder and hope? Whether your motherhood came through adoption or other means, God designed the wait for the birth of a child. Do you think the waiting you are experiencing now is wasted, or can God use it to change you for the better.

➡️ **According to this passage, what does hope do?**

Hope helps us wait! In other words, when you fix your eyes on God and not your child's circumstances, waiting will not cause your faith to unravel. Like the months-long wait for your child to join you, you wait for a spectacular end result. Your hope in God keeps you buoyed.

➡️ **How should you wait?**

Patience is key to our faith walk. Patience matches our steps to God's. It enables us to hear Him more clearly, trust Him more surely.

Still, depending on the circumstances of your child, waiting can be excruciating. God understands this. When you're so confused or distressed you don't even know how to pray, according to this passage who forms your prayers?

Imagine! The God who formed you, who knows you better than you know yourself, will even form your agonized prayers for your children in the midst of your heartache.

And then comes God's wonderful promise, which is why you can wait patiently for Him. You can trust Him with your heart's desire, as you set your expectations aside and hold out your hands in eager anticipation of how He is going to work in your child's life.

➡️ **Write a simple prayer in regard to your child based on the above verses. Thank God for all He is doing during this waiting period you are enduring. Reaffirm your trust in His plan and His schedule.**

**"So do not fear, for I am with you; do not be dismayed, for I am your God. I will strengthen you and help you; I will uphold you with my righteous right hand."**

## Praying Scripture – MYSELF

▶ Father, thank you for the confidence that if I ask anything according to your will, you hear me. (1 John 5:14-15)

▶ Thank you Father, that as I wait on you, you will renew my strength. I will soar on wings like eagles, I will run and not grow weary, I will walk and not be faint. (Isaiah 40:31)

▶ Father, I will wait for you; I will be strong and take heart and wait for you. (Psalm 27:14)

## Praying Scripture – MY CHILD

▶ Lord, let my child know that you are good; you are a refuge in times of trouble. Let him know that you care for those who trust in you. (Nahum 1:7)

▶ Father, when my child walks in the midst of trouble, preserve her life; stretch out your hand against the anger of her enemies and save her with your right hand. (Psalm 138:7)

▶ Father, let my child know that his help comes from you, the Maker of Heaven and Earth. (Psalm 121:2)

▶ Father, watch over my child's coming and going both now and forevermore. (Psalm 121:8)

# REFLECTIONS
REFLECTIONS

God has strengthened my confidence in Him by...

Today, I'm trusting these characteristics of God...

# Our Waiting—God Working

 **S**arah knew the frustration of waiting. God promised her and Abraham descendants too numerous to count, yet Sarah could not conceive. When I put myself in Sarah's shoes, it's easy to understand the anguish she felt over her childless home. *Why would God give them the promise of a child and then not deliver?* (see Genesis 12-21)

Many mothers, including myself, cling to Proverbs 22:6 in regard to their adult children.

Have you ever felt like God forgot about those words in regard to your child? Are you tired of waiting for this verse to come true? Sarah would understand you!

Sadly, during the years she waited for God to fulfill His promise, Sarah made a subtle, but very critical mistake. She placed her trust in the *promise* of God, rather than in God Himself. Thus her faith became dependent on how God kept that promise.

Sarah's decision left her at the mercy of her limited perception of what she thought possible. When it was no longer biologically possible for Sarah to have children, she began to look for a way to help God.

Do you see the difference, the danger, in where you put your faith? If your faith depends on how you expect God to answer your prayers, rather than on God Himself—regardless of what happens—you will begin to question God rather than trust Him. And then you will be tempted to help Him according to your comparatively limited ability.

On the other hand, if you release your idea of what your answered prayer should look like, and place your faith in God's character, you will move into the realm of *God's* ability—*and with God anything is possible.*

Like Sarah, when we get so focused on what *isn't*, our view toward our relationship with God gets skewed. Because we know that our prayers for our child's spiritual well-being can be fully within God's will, we look for ways to assist God. This can sometimes result in working against our prayers and our child moving in the opposite direction.

➡️ **When have you been guilty of giving God a helping hand in regard to your child's spiritual welfare?**

⮕ **What was the result?**

⮕ **"Take delight in the Lᴏʀᴅ, and he will give you the desires of your heart."**

—**Psalm 37:4**

Think about that verse for a minute. Read it over several times.

⮕ **What is the desire of your heart regarding your child?**

⮕ **What does this verse say you need to do in order to see your heart's desire fulfilled?**

It's astoundingly simple, isn't it? Delight in God! That's it! Your child's spiritual welfare rests in God's hands, just as Sarah's ability to have a child was in God's hands. The part you play in this scenario is to delight in the Lord!

The word "delight" comes from a Hebrew word meaning soft and pliable. To delight in God you must make yourself pliable in His hands. Have you seen those photos of a little girl standing on her father's feet as he dances her around the room? I think that's a perfect picture of what delighting in God looks like. Our feet standing on His feet, our hands held by His hands. Every move we make is His move, perfectly in sync with Him, delighting in dancing together.

Close your eyes for a moment. Picture God taking your hands and helping you put your feet on His feet. Now imagine the music beginning as the two of you move around the room. Can you feel what it means to delight in God?

➡️ **Write down your thoughts.**

Let go of your dreams for your child and devote yourself to delighting in God. Entrust your child's relationship with God to God. Stay out of His way and let Him work. A miracle is in the making.

**Scripture Focus: Psalms 27:14**

**"Wait for the Lord; be strong and take heart and wait for the Lord."**

## Praying Scripture – MYSELF

▸ Father, I know I will find rest in you alone; my hope comes from you. (Psalms 62:5)

▸ Thank you, Father, that your way is perfect; your word is flawless. You are my Shield and I take refuge in you. (Psalms 18:30)

▸ Lord, I will hold unswervingly to the hope I profess, for you are faithful. (Hebrews 10:23)

## Praying Scripture – MY CHILD

▸ Father, fulfill your purpose in my child; let her know that your love, O Lord, endures forever—do not abandon the works of your hands regarding my child. (Psalms 138:8)

▸ Father, I look forward to the day I will say, "Surely this is my God; I trusted in Him, and He saved my child. This is the Lord, my child trusted in Him; let us rejoice and be glad in His salvation." (Isaiah 25:9)

# REFLECTIONS
REFLECTIONS

_____
_____
_____
_____
_____
_____
_____

God has strengthened my confidence in Him by...

_____
_____
_____
_____
_____
_____

Today, I'm trusting these characteristics of God...

_____
_____
_____
_____
_____
_____
_____
_____

# The End of Waiting

Monica, the mother of one beloved child, delighted in her son's bright intelligence and his early dedication to God. As a teenager, however, Augustine began to stray from his spiritual and moral upbringing. Between his 17th and 28th years, he embraced immorality with abandon. He fathered a child outside of marriage, and even went so far as to join a cult that denounced the existence of God.

Monica was devastated. She began beating on the doors of heaven, pleading for God to intervene, but her prayers seemed unanswered. In desperation she went to her pastor, and with tears streaming down her face, begged him to talk to her son. He refused her request, assuring her that in God's time, Augustine would turn from his destructive path.

Refusing to leave, Monica continued to beg and weep. Pushed to his limits, her pastor spoke harshly, "Go, go! Leave me alone. Live on as you are living. It is not possible that the son of such tears should be lost."

Can you relate to Monica's desperate sorrow? Do you keep hoping to find just-the-right person or just-the-right book or just-the-right video that will cause your child to become spiritually engaged with God?

 **Write out your thoughts.**

Mixed with despair over our child's spiritual welfare often includes another element altogether: Pride.

We look at others' adult children who are passionate about God, and we feel a debilitating sense of failure and even shame. Then secondary concerns distract us: *What will people think? How am I going to explain my child's behavior and choices to my friends?*

These thoughts produce no good fruit and build a barrier in our own spiritual welfare as our focus moves from our Savior to ourselves.

**⇒ How has pride shown itself in your situation?**

Monica struggled with these same feelings and never stopped bombarding Heaven on her son's behalf. When her son turned 29, he made a decision that caused her the greatest despair yet. He decided to move to Rome, which at one time was known to be a city steeped in sin. Monica feared his geographic distance would equate to his spiritual distance from God.

The day of his departure, Monica accompanied him to the boat docks, all the while pleading with God to change her son's mind. When his ship's departure was delayed, Monica's heart soared, convinced God was answering her prayers.

Oh, how quick we can be to pounce on every occurrence as a "sign" that God is answering our prayers in the way we think He should. Unwittingly, we attach our faith to what we see. Like Monica, our hopes soar, only to have them dashed when nothing significant changes.

**⇒ When have you jumped to a conclusion about God's work in your child's life that wasn't accurate?**

At the docks, the heat of the hot summer day began to take its toll on Monica. Augustine convinced her to wait inside a nearby church, where it was cooler. Sitting in the cool interior, Monica leaned her head against the wall and fell asleep. Several hours later, she awoke with a start, panic gripping her. She ran from the church and down to the ship dock, only to discover the ship had departed. Her son hadn't even bothered to say goodbye. God seemed to have ignored the most desperate prayer to ever leave her lips.

Of course, the story does not end there. God *didn't* answer the prayer of Monica's lips—that her son not depart for Rome—but He *did* answer the prayer of her heart— that he return to Jesus Christ. It was in Rome that Augustine came back to God!

Today, 14 centuries later, we all benefit from that one mother's determined prayers, because Augustine went on to become a staunch defender of the truth and of faith. Thanks largely to him, the author of *The City of God* and *Confessions*, known to some as St. Augustine, that the light of the New Testament continued burning during the Dark Ages.

Never forget, as you pray for your child, that God is always working, even when His hand is not evident!

## Scripture Focus: Ephesians 1:18-21

**"I pray that the eyes of your heart may be enlightened in order that you may know the hope to which he has called you, the riches of his glorious inheritance in his holy people, and his incomparably great power for us who believe. That power is the same as the mighty strength he exerted when he raised Christ from the dead and seated him at his right hand in the heavenly realms, far above all rule and authority, power and dominion, and every name that is invoked, not only in the present age but also in the one to come."**

## Praying Scripture – MYSELF

▶ Thank you, Lord, that you are a Sun and Shield; that you bestow favor and honor; that you will withhold no good thing from those whose walk is blameless. (Psalms 84:11)

▶ Father, I will not throw away my confidence; I know it will be richly rewarded. I know that patient endurance is what I need now, so that I will continue to do your will. I will receive all that you have promised. (Hebrews 10:35-36)

## Praying Scripture – MY CHILD

▶ Father, make all grace abound to my child so that in all things, at all times he will have all that he needs, and will abound in every good work. (2 Corinthians 9:8)

▶ Thank you, Father, that neither death nor life, neither angels nor demons, neither the present nor the future, nor any powers, neither height nor depth, nor anything else in all creation, will be able to separate my child from your love. (Romans 8:38-39)

▶ Father, pour out your Spirit on my child, and your blessing on my descendants. (Isaiah 44:3)

# REFLECTIONS

_God has strengthened my confidence in Him by..._

_Today, I'm trusting these characteristics of God..._

# GOD'S
## amazing sovereignty

## Faithfulness Has Eternal Impact

**K**ing David loved God. His passion for God never dimmed. And, David sinned. He gave in to temptation and sin which displeased God. Still, his faithfulness to God defined him.

However, David's family was a mess! His children made decisions that broke his heart. Absalom went so far as to try to steal the throne from his father, plotting against his father's life, and desecrating his household. All the while, David's heart yearned for his wayward son.

Another son, Solomon, after getting off to a spectacular start that would have made any parent proud, later walked away from God. When Solomon persisted in his betrayal, God told him something that has great importance for us as mothers. Read 1 Kings 11:11-13:

➡ **"So the Lord said to Solomon, 'Since this is your attitude and you have not kept my covenant and my decrees, which I commanded you, I will most certainly tear the kingdom away from you and give it to one of your subordinates. Nevertheless, for the sake of David your father, I will not do it during your lifetime. I will tear it out of the hand of your son. Yet I will not tear the whole kingdom from him, but will give him one tribe for the sake of David my servant and for the sake of Jerusalem, which I have chosen.'"**

➡ **What phrase is repeated twice in this brief passage?**

Think about that. Solomon, a faithless man, nevertheless benefited from his *father's* faithfulness! Although he deserved to have his kingdom removed, God did not do it during his lifetime. *David's faithfulness resulted in mercy for his wayward child.*

It isn't just Solomon who benefitted from David's faithfulness. You can find that phrase repeated in the recorded biographies of several of David's descendants. As these kings turned away from God, each was shown mercy for David's sake.

⮞ **How have you benefited from the faithfulness of someone in your family or community?**

I cannot think of a better reason to walk in faithfulness than knowing it will impact my children and my children's children. Think of it! Your faithfulness significantly influences your family—long after you've ceased to exist on this Earth. For those of you with control issues, this should make you really happy!

I love all the instances in the Bible when an entire family is saved through one person's faithfulness. Take a look at Genesis 7:1:

⮞ **"The LORD then said to Noah, 'Go into the ark, you and your whole family, because I have found you righteous in this generation.'"**

And Joshua 6:25:

⮞ **"But Joshua spared Rahab the prostitute, with her family and all who belonged to her, because she hid the men Joshua had sent as spies to Jericho."**

Additionally, I find some compelling examples in the New Testament as they speak directly to our salvation only found in Jesus Christ. For example, there is Acts 16:31b:

⮞ **"Believe in the LORD Jesus, and you will be saved—you and your household."**

And Acts 11:13b-14:

⮞ **"Send to Joppa for Simon who is called Peter. He will bring you a message through which you and all your household will be saved."**

While these verses should not be taken as universal promises for every situation, they do clearly speak to a principle of faithfulness. Your salvation story and your faithfulness can, and should, make a difference in the lives of those around you.

Faithfulness is contagious.

Faithfulness is influential.

Faithfulness has eternal impact.

The effects of our faithfulness may not show right this moment; nevertheless, be assured God is doing a far greater work than we can imagine!

**➡ When do you find your faithfulness challenged?**

One final thought on faithfulness: In her book, *Prodigals and Those Who Love Them*, Ruth Bell Graham tells about using John 17 as a prayer for her son, Franklin, during a difficult time in his life. It is the same prayer Jesus prayed just before His crucifixion. As she prayed, verse 19 caught her attention: "For them I sanctify myself, that they too may be truly sanctified."

As she prayed that verse, Ruth wrote that she realized that for her son's sake, she needed to recommit her life to God before she could ask God to do it for Franklin. "It is unrealistic to ask the Lord to do in someone else's life that which we are unwilling for Him to do in ours."

As we daily surrender to the Lord and commit our lives to Him fully, our children will benefit. Your relationship with God matters. Your faithfulness to Him matters.

**"And without faith it is impossible to please God, because anyone who comes to him must believe that he exists and that he rewards those who earnestly seek him."**

---

### Praying Scripture – MYSELF

▶ Father, I pray in confidence knowing that if I ask anything according to your will, you hear me. (1 John 5:14)

▶ How wonderful to know, Lord, that even when my faith is as small as a mustard seed, I can say to this mountain, "Move from here to there," and it will move. Nothing is impossible for you. (Matthew 17:20)

▶ Lord, I know that everything is possible for the one who believes. (Mark 9:23)

▶ Father, I do believe; help me overcome my unbelief! (Mark 9:24)

### Praying Scripture – MY CHILD

▶ Thank you, Lord, that even when my child is faithless, you remain faithful. (2 Timothy 2:13)

▶ Father, let my child acknowledge her sin to you and not cover up her iniquity, so you will forgive my child's sin. (Psalm 32:5)

# REFLECTIONS

REFLECTIONS

God has strengthened my confidence in Him by...

Today, I'm trusting these characteristics of God...

# REFLECTIONS
REFLECTIONS

**PRAYER** WORTH REPEATING

# Standing on Holy Ground

I n Joshua 5, an exciting concept comes to light. The children of Israel have at last *entered* the long-awaited Promised Land, but not yet *taken possession* of it. The land still belongs to their enemies. However, God's reputation precedes the Israelites, so much so that their enemies shrink away from them in fear. Nevertheless, the cold hard truth is that this nation camps on enemy soil. Right now they can see the impenetrable and daunting walls of Jericho.

As Joshua stares out over this scene, out of nowhere, a Man with a drawn sword appears in front of him (vs. 13). Put yourself in this picture for a minute. In the heart of enemy territory, you stare at the massive walls surrounding an enemy city. Do you imagine your nerves would be on high alert?

Suddenly, without warning, you find yourself face-to-face with a Man holding a sword, ready for battle.

**How might you respond? What conclusions might you jump to?**

Joshua's first response is to ask the Man whose side He's on. "'Neither,' he replied, 'but as commander of the army of the LORD I have now come.'" (see vs. 13-14)

Joshua's second response is to fall facedown to the ground in reverence and ask, "…'What message does my LORD have for his servant?'" (vs. 14).

"The Commander of the LORD's army replied, 'Take off your sandals, for the place where you are standing is holy.'" And Joshua obeyed. (see vs. 15)

Two things strike me about the Man's answer. The first: He said He wasn't on either side! Does that surprise you? Wouldn't you assume that if He was Commander of the Lord's army, He would be on the side of the Israelites? It makes me wonder about the line we have drawn between ourselves and the world—and the attitudes we form around that line. How does God view that separation we create?

When an attitude of judgment creeps into our lives unnoticed, the barrier it erects devastates. John 3:17 sets the guideline for how we should live in order to draw people to Christ:

➡ **"For God did not send his Son into the world to condemn the world, but to save the world through him."**

Consider your own life. Might the line between yourself and the world limit your impact on the people you come in contact with? Does it limit the impact you have on your child?

➡ **What are some things you say or do that might create a barrier to your child's response to God?**

Take some time right now and ask God to open your eyes to any lines of judgment you have drawn which prevent you from embracing those for whom Christ gave His life. Next, ask Him to forgive you for any barrier you created and then, to help you tear it down.

The second thing that strikes me in this passage: the Man told Joshua to remove his sandals because he stood on holy ground. Right there in the middle of enemy territory (and this enemy worshipped despicable gods), the ground was holy because of the presence of God! Take a moment and consider the implications of God's presence making even desecrated ground holy.

Wherever God is, the ground is holy—and God can go anywhere!

There is no physical or emotional barrier He can't overcome.

There is no philosophy or belief He can't overpower.

There is no circumstance He cannot transform.

You are limited, but *God is not*.

There is something else without limits. Your prayers! Your prayers unite you with God as He works in places you cannot visit. Your prayers partner you with God in circumstances far beyond your reach. Remember, *where God is, the ground is holy*. Holiness walks hand-in-hand with the miraculous. Impenetrable walls crumble in the presence of the Holy. When God is present for your child, the ground she is standing on becomes holy ground.

➡️ **Take some time to worship Almighty God, who has no limitations.**

**Scripture Focus: John 14:12**

**"Very truly I tell you, whoever believes in me will do the works I have been doing, and they will do even greater things than these, because I am going to the Father."**

## Praying Scripture – MYSELF

▶ Father, I will be glad and rejoice in your love, for you see my affliction and know the anguish of my soul. (Psalm 31:7)

▶ Father, thank you that in all things I am more than a conqueror through you who love me. (Romans 8:37)

## Praying Scripture – MY CHILD

▶ Lord, I ask that you will set my child free and then he will be free indeed. (John 8:36)

▶ Father, let my child love you with all her heart and with all her soul and with all her mind and with all her strength. (Mark 12:30)

▶ Father, I ask that my child will obey you, and that you will be his God and that he will be your child. Let him walk in all the ways you command, so that it may go well with him. (Jeremiah 7:23)

▶ Lord, let my child love you and keep your commands. (John 14:15)

▶ Lord, I pray that my child will pay attention to your commands, so that her peace will be like a river, and her well-being like the waves of the sea. (Isaiah 48:18)

# REFLECTIONS
REFLECTIONS

_____
_____
_____
_____
_____
_____
_____
_____

God has strengthened my confidence in Him by...

_____
_____
_____
_____
_____
_____
_____

God has strengthened my confidence in Him by...

_____
_____
_____
_____
_____
_____
_____

# No One Can Thwart the Will of God

The book of Esther enthralls readers like few books of the Bible. Esther serves as the inspiration for many of the "happily-ever-after" fairy tales you've read as a child. But this Old Testament story is no fairy tale. It is one-hundred-percent true and delights the hearts of all its readers. Tucked in at the very end of the account sits a powerful truth for mothers. If you recall, the story tells of when an evil man named Haman convinces King Xerxes to pass a law stating that all Jews living in Persia could be exterminated on a certain day. During this time in history, Persian law could never be set aside—not even by the king himself.

Later in the book, when the king comes to his senses and realizes the treachery of Haman, he then orders Haman hanged. However, the law regarding the Jews remained in effect and could not be repealed. So the king allows a new edict. This one, recorded in Esther 8:11, permitted Jews to defend themselves on the day they were to be annihilated:

➡ **"The king's edict granted the Jews in every city the right to assemble and protect themselves; to destroy, kill and annihilate the armed men of any nationality or province who might attack them and their women and children, and to plunder the property of their enemies."**

Here is the truth for us as parents. Sometimes our children make decisions that set things in motion we cannot undo, no matter how much we wish we could. Our powerlessness to stop the resulting chain of events leaves us no choice but to see them through—just as the order against the Jews could not be stopped.

Nevertheless, the outcome remains in God's control. Even in miserable circumstances, God keeps our child's best interest at heart.

Because of this sure knowledge, we can realize a joyful anticipation even before we know how the story ends. The Jews of Esther's day surely did, as we see in Esther 8:13-17:

➡ **"A copy of the text of the edict was to be issued as law in every province and made known to the people of every nationality so that the Jews would be ready on that day to avenge themselves on their enemies.**

"The couriers, riding the royal horses, went out, spurred on by the king's command, and the edict was issued in the citadel of Susa.

"When Mordecai left the king's presence, he was wearing royal garments of blue and white, a large crown of gold and a purple robe of fine linen. And the city of Susa held a joyous celebration. For the Jews it was a time of happiness and joy, gladness and honor. In every province and in every city to which the edict of the king came, there was joy and gladness among the Jews, with feasting and celebrating. And many people of other nationalities became Jews because fear of the Jews had seized them."

**Who else in the Bible trusts God with this kind of abandon?**

This example shows the exact same level of trust we saw in Gideon—the Jews began celebrating before the outcome was known! The appointed day of their slaughter remained. Nothing changed about that. They had to see it through. And yet they rejoiced because their trust in God was unshakable! They danced in the streets and held celebratory feasts, as they showed exuberant joy. Oh, how quickly God can turn the tables!

Do not waste your energy and sabotage your trust by giving in to dismay over the choices your child makes and the circumstances set in motion by these choices. Focus instead on God. He remains sovereign, even in the midst of these circumstances. Your unwavering trust in God, despite the truth of your child's situation, is not misplaced. For reassurance, read Esther 9:1-2:

**"On the thirteenth day of the twelfth month, the month of Adar, the edict commanded by the king was to be carried out. On this day the enemies of the Jews had hoped to overpower them, but now the tables were turned and the Jews got the upper hand over those who hated them. The Jews assembled in their cities in all the provinces of King Xerxes to attack those determined to destroy them. No one could stand against them, because the people of all the other nationalities were afraid of them."**

Is this not amazing? The tables are turned! The losers become the winners! And here's the eternal magnificence—the God who was looking out for the Jews in Esther's day is the very same God who is looking out for your child. Your hope is that one day the tables will be turned in your child's life as well. Whatever circumstances your child is in right now, whatever circumstances show up tomorrow—know that they are never out of God's control. No matter what reality faces you, this is not the time to give in to worry or fear. This is a time to celebrate! Rejoice in God, who knows exactly what He's doing and who has your child's best interests at heart. Be filled with joyful anticipation as you allow God to work in His way and in His time. When you start to doubt, remember Proverbs 3:5-6:

▶ **"Trust in the Lord with all your heart and lean not on your own understanding; in all your ways submit to him, and he will make your paths straight."**

**Scripture Focus: Psalms 34:8-9**

**"Taste and see that the Lord is good; blessed is the one who takes refuge in him. Fear the Lord, you his holy people, for those who fear him lack nothing."**

## Praying Scripture – MYSELF

▶ Thank You, Father, for the exceeding greatness of your power toward those who believe according to the working of your mighty power. (Ephesians 1:19)

▶ Thank you, Father, that you are able to do exceedingly abundantly above all that I ask or think, according to your power that works in me. (Ephesians 3:20)

▶ Father, I know your grace is sufficient for me, and your strength is made perfect in my weakness. (2 Corinthians 12:9)

▶ Father, I will be strong and courageous. I will not be afraid; I will not be discouraged, for you, my God, will be with me wherever I go. (Joshua 1:9)

## Praying Scripture – MY CHILD

▶ Father, teach my child to walk by faith and not by sight. (2 Corinthians 5:7)

▶ Father, let my child fight the good fight of faith. Let her take hold of the eternal life to which she was called. (1 Timothy 6:12)

▶ Lord, let my child have faith in you. (Mark 11:22)

# REFLECTIONS
REFLECTIONS

God has strengthened my confidence in Him by...

Today, I'm trusting these characteristics of God...

# Nevertheless
# I WILL PRAY

MOTHER                                              CHILD

_____              _____
_____              _____
_____              _____
_____              _____
_____              _____
_____              _____
_____              _____
_____              _____
_____              _____
_____              _____
_____              _____
_____              _____
_____              _____
_____              _____
_____              _____
_____              _____
_____              _____
_____              _____
_____              _____
_____              _____
_____              _____
_____              _____
_____              _____
_____              _____

# God's Pursuing Love

**God, who created the universe, is full of love and mercy.
He desires for you to personally receive His love and mercy.**

It does not matter what has happened in your past. No matter what you've done. No matter how you've lived your life. God's mercy is greater. God understands you—your hopes, your dreams, your frustrations, your loneliness, your heartaches. His love caused Him to pursue us, to leave Heaven and come to Earth.

> **For this is how God loved the world: He gave his one and only Son, so that everyone who believes in him will not perish but have eternal life. God sent his Son into the world not to judge the world, but to save the world through him.**
>
> **—John 3:16-17**

**God is love.
He is a God of relationship.**

God created us to have a real and personal relationship with Him. However, we chose another path—one that does not honor God. That's the essence of what the Bible calls sin. All of us carry sin's consequence—sin keeps us from having a loving relationship with God.

But God loves so deeply that *He* closed that gap of separation. Jesus Christ is God. He decided to come after us—to pursue us! He came to Earth to live the perfect life with no sin, and then to die in our place—taking the punishment for our sin. Jesus did all the work for us.

Nothing *we* can do will bring us closer to God. No good works. No good deeds. No avoidance of evil.

> **For God made Christ, who never sinned, to be the offering for our sin, so that we could be made right with God through Christ.**
>
> **—2 Corinthians 5:21**

> **But God is so rich in mercy, and he loved us so much, that even though we were dead because of our sins, he gave us life when he raised Christ from the dead. (It is only by God's grace that you have been saved!)**
>
> **—Ephesians 2:4-5**

Jesus Christ paid the penalty for sin on the cross. But He did not stay dead! He came back to life. He rose from the dead. And He is ready to share His life with you.

**Jesus is alive today.**
**He offers reconciliation to us.**
**He can give you a new beginning and a newly created life.**

➡ **This means that anyone who belongs to Christ has become a new person. The old life is gone; a new life has begun!**

**—2 Corinthians 5:17**

## How do you begin this new life?

Place your trust in Jesus Christ. Believe that He is God. Receive the love He has for you. Agree with God about your sin and believe that Jesus came to reconcile you to a relationship with God. He closed the separation between you through His life, death, and resurrection. Ask Jesus Christ to lead your life.

When you trust Jesus Christ, He will live in your life. His Spirit will live inside you. The Holy Spirit will help you to live a life that honors Him.

Would you like to begin this new life? You can start today with a few simple words like "Dear Jesus, I believe that You are God and that You love me and came to reconcile us."

**Or pray something like this:**

**Jesus, I believe you are the Son of God and that you died on the cross to pay the penalty for my sin. Forgive me. I turn away from my sin and choose to live a life that honors you.**

**I want to follow you and make you the leader of my life.**

**Thank you for your gift of eternal life and for the Holy Spirit, who has now come to live in me. I ask this in your name. Amen**

(Scripture referenced in God's Pursuing Love came from the New Living Translation of the Bible)

Stonecroft would like to offer you a free download of *A New Beginning*, a short Bible study that will help you as you begin your new relationship with God. Please visit **stonecroft.org/newbeginning**.

# REFLECTIONS

# REFLECTIONS

# REFLECTIONS

REFLECTIONS

# REFLECTIONS

## Special Thanks

Stonecroft offers special thanks to Janice Mayo Mathers, the primary author of *Prayer Worth Repeating*. The mother of two adult children, Janice faithfully prays and trusts God to move in and through their lives. Janice is married and lives in Oregon.

# Stonecroft Resources

Stonecroft Bible Studies and other resources make the Word of God accessible to everyone. Stonecroft studies allow small groups to discover the adventure of a personal relationship with God and introduce others to God's unlimited love, grace, forgiveness, and power. To learn more, visit **stonecroft.org/store**.

### Make Us One

Gather together a small group of women to learn from the Bible and pray for your marriages. Each chapter in Make Us One includes biblical teaching, practical illustrations, Scripture-saturated prayer, and a place to record your reflections. Invest in your marriage with Make Us One— and discover a life-transforming relationship with God!

### Today I Pray

When we bow before God on behalf of someone who doesn't yet know of His saving work, of His great love in sending His Son Jesus, of His mercy and goodness, we enter into a work that has eternal impact. Stonecroft designed Today I Pray as a 30-day intercessory prayer commitment that you may use to focus your prayers on behalf of a specific person, or to pray for many—because your prayers are powerful and important!

### Prayer—Talking with God

This booklet provides insight and biblical principles to help you establish a stronger, more effective prayer life.

### Prayer Journal

A practical resource to strengthen your prayer life, this booklet includes an introductory section about the importance of prayer, the basic elements of prayer, and a clear Gospel presentation, as well as 40 pages of journaling your prayer requests and God's answers.

## Connecting with God (8 chapters)

Prayer is our heart-to-heart communication with our heavenly Father. This study examines the purpose, power, and elements of prayer, sharing biblical principles for effective prayer.

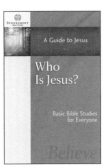

## Who is Jesus? (6 chapters)

He was a rebel against the status quo. The religious community viewed Him as a threat. The helpless and outcast considered Him a friend. Explore the life and teachings of Jesus—this rebel with a cause who challenges us today to a life of radical faith.

## What is God Like? (6 chapters)

What is God like? Is He just a higher power? Has He created us and left us on our own? Where is He when things don't make sense? Discover what the Bible tells us about God and how we can know Him in a life-transforming way.

## Who is the Holy Spirit? (6 chapters)

Are you living up to the full life that God wants for you? Learn about the Holy Spirit, our Helper and power source for everyday living, who works in perfect harmony with God the Father and Jesus the Son.

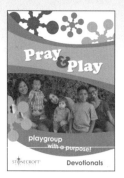

**Pray & Play Devotional** (12 devotions)

It's playgroup with a purpose! Plus Mom tips. For details on starting a Pray & Play group, visit stonecroft.org/prayandplay or call 800.525.8627.

**Aware** (5 chapters)

Making Jesus known every day starts when we are Aware of those around us. This dynamic Stonecroft Small Group Bible Study about "Always Watching and Responding with Encouragement" equips and engages people in the initial steps to the joys of evangelism.

**Belong** (6 chapters)

For many in today's culture, the desire to belong is often part of their journey to believe. Belong explores how we can follow in Jesus' footsteps—and walk with others on their journey to belong.

**Call** (7 chapters)

Every day we meet people without Christ. That is God's intention. He wants His people to initiate and build friendships. He wants us together. Call helps us take a closer look at how God makes Himself known through our relationships with those around us. Discover together God's clear calling for you and those near to you.

**Order these and other Stonecroft Resources at our online store**
# stonecroft.org/store or call 888.819.5218
**When placing an order by phone, please identify yourself as a Stonecroft customer.**

# Stonecroft

where she is ✛ as she is

**Stonecroft staff and volunteers work together to take the Gospel of Jesus Christ to each woman where she is, as she is.**

## ➡️ Relevant

Join Stonecroft to share the Good News in relevant ways with women in your community.

> **"I'm indebted to Stonecroft for being there at the right time for me to hear about Jesus."**
>
> **— Janet Meyers, Fort Wayne, Indiana**

## ➡️ Community

Join a movement bigger than you'd ever imagine—yet experience genuine local community as Stonecroft's world-wide network of more than 25,000 women train, equip, and support each other to effectively share the Gospel.

## ➡️ Impact

We make a difference today and through eternity by introducing women to the One who created them.

➡️ **"Many of [them] from that town believed in him because of the woman's testimony..." —John 4:39, NIV**

**Confidently take the Good News of Jesus Christ to each woman where she is—not expecting her to come to you, and as she is— no matter her circumstance or background.**

**Email connections@stonecroft.org Visit stonecroft.org**

> **"I'm still completely amazed at what God has chosen to do through me!"**
>
> **— Maria Diedrich Lopez Arvada, CO**

Share the Good News with your friends, neighbors, and co-workers—with women who need to begin a relationship with their Creator God through His Son, Jesus Christ.

We equip and encourage women in thousands of communities to take the Gospel to women where they are, as they are. Join us today.

Stonecroft Outreach—sets the stage for women to hear the Gospel in relevant large-venue, seminar, or small-group settings. stonecroft.org

Stonecroft Prays!—calls women of all ages together to pray for effective avenues to reach today's women with the Gospel. stonecroft.org/prays

Stonecroft Military—honors women connected with the U.S. Military by delivering the Gospel through events and small groups. stonecroft.org/military

Stonecroft Bible Studies—introduces Jesus Christ as Savior and Lord though the power of scripture. stonecroft.org/store

Stonecroft Leader Development—provides training resources and tools to support women as they share the Gospel. stonecroft.org

stonecroft.org—offers fresh content to equip and encourage our volunteers. Visit us today to learn more and to connect with Stonecroft.

Make a difference. Make a difference in your community. Make a difference in another woman's life. Make a difference in your life. Make a difference for God's Kingdom.

Join Stonecroft today and bring the Gospel to each woman, where she is—not expecting her to come to you, and as she is— no matter her circumstance or background.

 Find us on Facebook  twitter

Get started:
connections@stonecroft.org
800.525.8627

Support Stonecroft:
stonecroft.org/donate
800.525.8627

Stonecroft Resources:
stonecroft.org/store
888.819.5218